Nadia Comaneci

Contents

Written by Sally Cole
Illustrated by Bruce Potter

Nadia as a Little Girl

Nadia Comaneci was born in 1961 in Onesti, in Romania. When Nadia was very small she was always climbing on things. As soon as Nadia could run, she ran everywhere.

When Nadia was three years old she went to kindergarten. At kindergarten, Nadia did all sorts of things. She played soccer and climbed trees. Nadia never sat still, she was always playing and running about.

Gymnastics Lessons

Nadia and her friends had gymnastics lessons at kindergarten. When Nadia was six years old, she had special coaching lessons in gymnastics.

Nadia's gymnastic coaches were called Bela and Marta Karoly. Marta Karoly had also been a gymnast. Marta taught the little girls not to be scared of falling. Bela was strong, and he was always there to catch the little girls if they fell.

Nadia at Gymnastics High School

Nadia went to school when she was six and a half years old but she still had gymnastics lessons. When Nadia was eight years old, she went to a special Gymnastics High School.

At the special Gymnastics High School, Nadia still had to go to her reading and writing lessons. She spent four and a half hours in the classroom and four hours in the gym. But Nadia did not just do her lessons and gymnastics, she also learned ballet. The ballet lessons showed Nadia how to be graceful.

Competitions

Nadia's first big gymnastics competition was for girls under the age of ten. Nadia was nine. She was in a team with five other little girls. This competition was an international competition. Nadia's team did very well and won.

Because it was an international competition, Nadia competed against children from other countries in the world.

Nadia did very well at the competition. She scored 38.5 out of 40 points and her team won the competition.

At this competition, Nadia started to collect dolls. Every time she went to a competition in another country, she brought another new doll home with her.

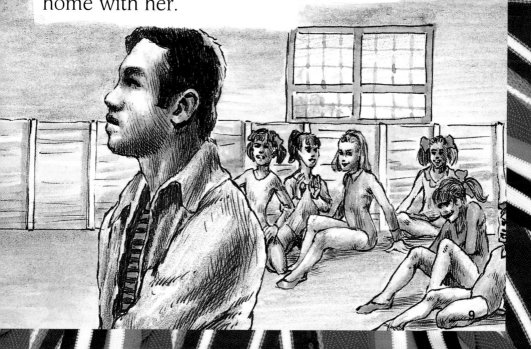

Nadia's Dream of the Olympics

When Nadia was ten years old, she told her coach she wanted to compete at the next Olympic Games. Only the best athletes in the world compete at the Olympic Games. So for the next four years, Nadia entered lots of competitions and worked very hard.

Nadia took part in another big gymnastics competition when she was eleven years old. Nadia and her team competed against gymnasts from the Soviet Union, East Germany, and Hungary.

Nadia and her friends were still very young to be entering international competitions.

Nadia worked very hard and she did very well on the bars and the beam at this competition. Nadia did so well that she won lots of medals. Nadia won three gold medals and one silver medal. She was very happy.

But Nadia could not stop there. She had to keep working hard if she wanted to be the very best gymnast in the world. Nadia worked hard. She trained every day. She entered and won lots more competitions. In 1976, Nadia was the Gymnastics Champion of Europe.

The 1976 Olympic Games

At the Montreal Olympic Games in Canada, Nadia made history. She became the youngest, and the first, gymnast to score 10 out of 10, and she did it seven times.

Nadia won gold medals in the all-round competition, the bars and the beam. Now, Nadia was the very best gymnast in the world.

Because of her win at the Olympic Games, Nadia became famous all round the world. Nadia had shown that a little girl with a will to win can be the best at what she chooses to do.

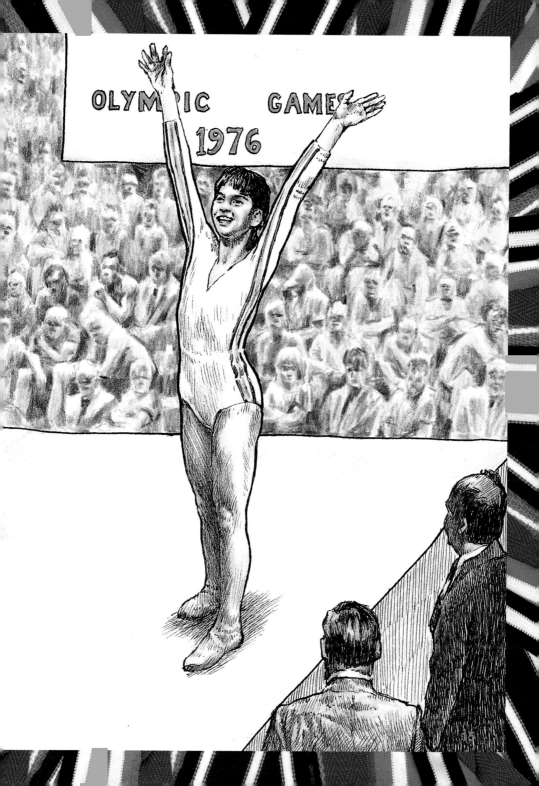

Index